Poverty and plenty

RUTH

by Tim Chester

Poverty and plenty
The Good Book Guide to Ruth
© Tim Chester/The Good Book Company, 2011. Reprinted 2014, 2016, 2018.

The Good Book Company
Tel (UK): 0333 123 0880
Tel (int): + (44) 208-942-0880
Tel: (US): 866 244 2165
Email: info@thegoodbook.co.uk

Websites
UK: www.thegoodbook.co.uk
N America: www.thegoodbook.com
Australia: www.thegoodbook.com.au
New Zealand: www.thegoodbook.co.nz

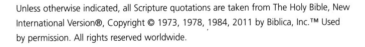

ISBN: 9781905564910

Printed in India

CONTENTS

Introduction: Good Book Guides

Every Bible-study group is different—yours may take place in a church building, in a home or in a cafe, on a train, over a leisurely mid-morning coffee or squashed into a 30-minute lunch break. Your group may include new Christians, mature Christians, non-Christians, mums and tots, students, businessmen or teens. That's why we've designed these *Good Book Guides* to be flexible for use in many different situations.

Our aim in each session is to uncover the meaning of a passage, and see how it fits into the "big picture" of the Bible. But that can never be the end. We also need to appropriately apply what we have discovered to our lives. Let's take a look at what is included:

⊕ **Talkabout:** Most groups need to "break the ice" at the beginning of a session, and here's the question that will do that. It's designed to get people talking around a subject that will be covered in the course of the Bible study.

⊥ **Investigate:** The Bible text for each session is broken up into manageable chunks, with questions that aim to help you understand what the passage is about. **The Leader's Guide** contains **guidance on questions**, and sometimes ⊠ additional "follow-up" questions.

⊡ **Explore more (optional):** These questions will help you connect what you have learned to other parts of the Bible, so you can begin to fit it all together like a jig-saw; or occasionally look at a part of the passage that's not dealt with in detail in the main study.

➔ **Apply:** As you go through a Bible study, you'll keep coming across **apply** sections. These are questions to get the group discussing what the Bible teaching means in practice for you and your church. ⊡ **Getting personal** is an opportunity for you to think, plan and pray about the changes that you personally may need to make as a result of what you have learned.

⬆ **Pray:** We want to encourage prayer that is rooted in God's word—in line with His concerns, purposes and promises. So each session ends with an opportunity to review the truths and challenges highlighted by the Bible study, and turn them into prayers of request and thanksgiving.

The **Leader's Guide** and introduction provide historical background information, explanations of the Bible texts for each session, ideas for **optional extra** activities, and guidance on how best to help people uncover the truths of God's word.

Why study Ruth?

What's so special about the story of Ruth? This woman was no powerful princess—just a young, vulnerable widow, an impoverished outcast. The story records no famous events or places—just an average family suffering misfortune, in a small agricultural community occupied with their livelihoods and customs.

But beneath the surface, the hidden hand of God is at work in the lives of these utterly ordinary people.

God transforms hardship from bitterness to joy; God's word liberates people to become a community filled with loving-kindness towards outcasts; God's people reach out to their enemies; men and women in troubled and chaotic times choose to do good and act rightly.

And, bigger than all of these, we see God's great plan for the whole world being played out in the lives of ordinary people. We discover that these ordinary events in the lives of ordinary people are part of a chain that ends with the coming of a promised Saviour-King to redeem people of all nations.

The whole story is a beautiful picture of Jesus our Redeemer, and the unimaginable difference He makes to people saved by Him.

Like those in this story, we are just ordinary folk, unable to see how the events of our lives will turn out. But by understanding God's wonderful sovereign purposes at work in the story of Ruth, we too can trust God and rejoice that our "poverty" will be turned to "plenty" by discovering the riches that are ours through Jesus Christ.

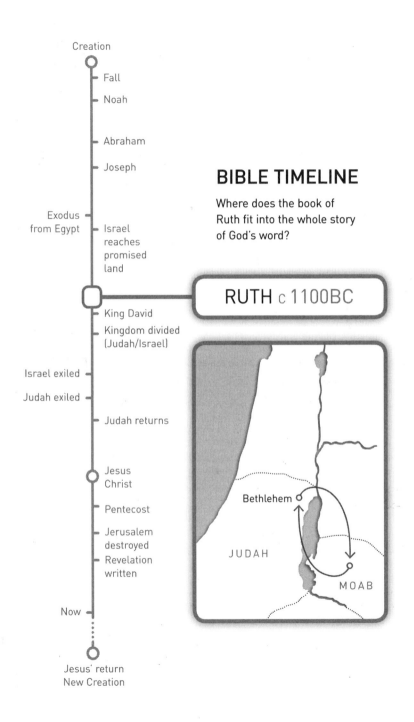

Creation

Fall

Noah

Abraham

Joseph

Exodus from Egypt

Israel reaches promised land

BIBLE TIMELINE

Where does the book of Ruth fit into the whole story of God's word?

RUTH c 1100BC

King David

Kingdom divided (Judah/Israel)

Israel exiled

Judah exiled

Judah returns

Jesus Christ

Pentecost

Jerusalem destroyed

Revelation written

Now

Jesus' return New Creation

Bethlehem

JUDAH

MOAB

1

Ruth 1 – 2

A HIDDEN HAND

⊕ talkabout

1. At what times in your life have you have found it hard to trust God?

> Lamar, Luke, First year of College, now.
> When I feel a lack of control.

⊕ investigate

> **Read Ruth 1**

2. How did Elimelek respond to famine?

> Went to moab, which they were not suppose to do.

3. **Look at Deuteronomy 32 v 15-18, 23-24, 36-39.** How should the people of Israel have understood their famine? How should they have responded?

> understood it was because of their disobedience.

4. **Read Deuteronomy 23 v 3-6.** What was the problem with going to Moab and marrying Moabite women?

> They weren't suppose to because it was against the law, but ultimately, they worshipped other gods.

5. Imagine what going back with Naomi meant for Ruth.

> everything was foreign.
> never see her family
> again.

Seven times in chapter 1 God is called "the LORD" or "Yahweh". It is God's special covenant name with Israel. The word "kindness" in verse 8 means covenant love, loving-kindness or loyalty.

6. How does Ruth show the covenant love of the LORD in her attitude to Naomi?

> She stays with her.
> commits to suffering
> with her.

7. How does Naomi describe what has happened to her in v 20-21?

> wants to change her name
> to rep   it her sorrow
>   "bitter"

8. Who does Naomi blame her misfortune on? Was she right to do this?

> God. unclear if she's
> "referring to God's response to
> sin. or no connection.

➡ **apply**

9. **Read Romans 5 v 1-5.** What should hardship produce in our lives?

⊡ **getting personal**

Who do you blame for misfortune in your life? Do difficulties or setbacks make you bitter towards God? Or do they produce perseverance, character and hope?

⊕ **investigate**

In 1 v 21 Naomi says she comes back empty. But in 3 v 17 Boaz can say to Ruth: "Don't go back to your mother-in-law empty-handed."

In chapter 1 Naomi is bitter because she has lost her two sons.

But in chapter 4 the women of the village praise God "for your [Naomi's] daughter-in-law, who loves you and who is better to you than seven sons..." (4 v 15). The circumstances of Naomi and Ruth change round completely.

▶ **Read Ruth 2**

10. How do we see God's hand changing the circumstances of Naomi and Ruth?

In verse 1 we learn that Naomi has a rich relative. In verse 2 Ruth asks to glean in the fields of "anyone in whose eyes I find favour". Ruth is going to pick a random landowner, but verse 1 suggests this choice may not turn out to be random at all! Verse 3 says "as it turned out". We might translate this as "it just so happened". It seems as if Ruth got lucky. But the writer highlights the "big coincidences" in the life of Ruth to point to God's hidden hand. There is no "miracle", but with the writer's help we can see God's providential care.

11. **Look at verses 12 and 20.** What is said about the LORD in chapter 2?

⊡ apply

12. The writer gives us a glimpse of God's providence in the lives of Ruth and Naomi, but Ruth and Naomi do not see this as the story unfolds anymore than we usually do in our lives. What encouragement does this story give you for your circumstances?

13. Only in 2 v 20 does Naomi begin to put the pieces together and see God's hand at work. She is catching up with God's providence. Where can you see God's hand at work in your life?

⊡ pray

Compare 1 v 9 and 3 v 1 (see the NIV footnote). Prayer and providence interweave in the story of Ruth and in our stories. With this in mind, bring your needs to God in prayer.

Spend a few moments quietly thinking of the problems you face in your life. Slowly read aloud some or all of the following passages, giving people time to reflect on how these verses speak to their circumstances.

- Ruth 2 v 12
- Psalm 17 v 6-8
- Psalm 36 v 7-8
- Psalm 57 v 1
- Psalm 91 v 1-4
- Philippians 4 v 6-7

2 Ruth 2
A LIBERATING WORD

The story so far

Naomi and her Moabite daughter-in-law, Ruth, have returned to Israel. God rules over our lives, even through the suffering we experience. His providence is often hidden from us at the time.

⊕ talkabout

1. Recall an act of kindness that someone has done for you recently.

⊍ investigate

❯ Read Ruth 2

2. What threats did Ruth face as a widow and refugee in a strange country?

> **DICTIONARY**
>
> **Glean (v 2):** gathering left-over grain after the harvest.

3. **Read Deuteronomy 10 v 17-19.** Summarise what is commanded. How is this law fulfilled in the story of Ruth?

4. **Read Deuteronomy 24 v 19-22.** Summarise what is commanded. How is this law fulfilled in the story of Ruth?

5. What do we learn about the character of Ruth from these verses?

6. What do we learn about the character of Boaz from these verses?

7. In Ruth 2, how do we see people expressing loving-kindness that goes beyond the letter of the law?

optional

⊙ explore more

> **Read Deuteronomy 10 v 17-19**

Why does God say the Israelites should look after foreigners?

What was the rule of Egypt like for God's people?

What is the rule of God like for God's people and those who find refuge among them?

What does the law of God reveal about God?

The time of the Judges, when the story of Ruth takes place, was a time when God's law was ignored. "In those days Israel had no king; everyone did as they saw fit" (Judges 21 v 25). Judges 17 – 21 describe the moral chaos and evil this created. But it seems that in Bethlehem and in Boaz's house, the law was loved.

8. What kind of community does obedience to God create?

9. How does this fulfil God's promise to bless the nations through His people?

God is kind to Ruth and Naomi (v 12, 20), but He is kind to them through the kindness and obedience of His people.

⤳ apply

10. With men like Boaz, Bethlehem would have been an attractive community of kindness that many would like to be part of. What are the signs that the same is true of your Christian community?

⊡ getting personal

Think of three acts of kindness that you could do this week.

⬆ **pray**

"The Lord ... has not stopped showing his kindness" (Ruth 2 v 20).

• List some of the ways in which God has been kind to you.

• Give thanks to Him for these kindnesses with short one- or two-sentence prayers.

3
Ruth 2 – 3
A WELCOMING COMMUNITY

The story so far

Naomi and her Moabite daughter-in-law, Ruth, have returned to Israel. God rules over our lives, even through the suffering we experience. His providence is often hidden from us at the time.

They are desperately poor, but are shown love and kindness by a community that has been shaped by God's word.

⊕ talkabout

1. Describe a situation in which you felt like an outsider. How did it feel?

⊥ investigate

❯ Read Ruth 2 – 3

The background to this passage is found in Deuteronomy 25 v 5-10. If an Israelite man died without producing an heir, a relative was to marry his widow so that their first son could bear the name of the deceased man. Naomi realised that under this law Boaz could marry Ruth, providing for her daughter-in-law and continuing Elimelek's family name.

Boaz called Ruth "daughter", which suggests there was a significant age gap between them (2 v 8; 3 v 10-11). Ruth could have married a younger man

> **DICTIONARY**
>
> **Winnowing (3 v 2):** removing the outer husks from grain. Part of the process of preparing grain to make flour.
> **Redeem (v 9):** to buy back something that you previously owned.

(3 v 10), but she offered herself to Boaz out of covenant faithfulness to Naomi and her family.

We are not sure of the significance of raising the corner of Boaz's garment, but it seems to symbolise coming under his protection.

2. Imagine how Ruth and Boaz felt at each stage of the story.

3. How is Ruth described in 1 v 4, 22; 2 v 2, 6, 21; 4 v 5, 10? What is the significance of this?

4. How were Moabites viewed in Israel? (**See Deuteronomy 23 v 3-6.**)

5. How does Ruth view God's people? (See 1 v 16.)

According to 1 v 22: *"Naomi returned, and Ruth the Moabite her daughter-in-law with her, who returned from the country of Moab"* (ESV). Ruth "returned" to a place where she had never been (2 v 11)! The writer implies she is returning home—home to those who are now her people.

6. How do we see Ruth being included among God's people?

Ruth is an outsider. But she is welcomed into God's community. God's wings of refuge are found through inclusion in the covenant community as they are faithful to their covenant obligations in the spirit of covenant love. The word "home" in 3 v 1 is literally "rest". It is an image of salvation.

⮕ apply

7. What different attitudes do people have to refugees and immigrants?

8. What could you or your church do to provide a welcome for immigrants or other marginalised groups?

☺ getting personal

Think about your attitude to people whose background or personality is different from yours. Think about specific individuals. Could your attitude be described as loving-kindness? Does it reflect God's loving-kindness towards you?

⊡ investigate

9. The "garment" in 3 v 9 is the same word as "wings" in 2 v 12.
What is the significance of the parallels between these two verses?

10. Can you think of times when you have discovered that you are God's
answer to your prayer for someone?

⊡ explore more

▶ **Read Ezekiel 16 v 1-8**

Compare Ezekiel 16 v 8 and Ruth 3 v 9.

What do these parallels tell us about God's relationship with His people?

What do they tell us about our welcome to outsiders?

11. Ruth is not only a refugee. She is also a woman and a widow. Look at
1 v 21, 2 v 5 and 2 v 9. What do these verses tell us about the place of
women in that culture?

12. Look ahead to 4 v 15. What attitude about the value of women, counter cultural back then, is shown here?

⊡ explore more

optional

❯ Read Luke 5 v 27-32

Notice how Jesus welcomes the outsiders of His day.

What does the welcoming attitude of Jesus tell us about God?

Why are the Pharisees scandalised by the way Jesus includes "outsiders"?

➔ apply

13. Who are the outsiders in your area? What does your church do to ensure they feel welcome?

↑ pray

"May you be richly rewarded by the Lord, the God of Israel, under whose wings you have come to take refuge" (Ruth 2 v 12).

Use this prayer to pray for outsiders in your area.

Beware: Like Boaz, God may use you to be the answer to your own prayer!

4 Ruth 4
A FAITHFUL REDEEMER

The story so far

Naomi and her Moabite daughter-in-law, Ruth, have returned to Israel. God rules over our lives, even through the suffering we experience. His providence is often hidden from us at the time.

They are desperately poor, but are shown love and kindness by a community that has been shaped by God's word. Ruth has claimed her "rights" under the law of Israel to be redeemed as a widow by her relative Boaz. But will he do it?

⊕ talkabout

1. How much easier or harder is it for young Christians to live faithfully for Christ than it was for previous generations?

⊕ investigate

The story of Ruth takes place in a time of widespread unfaithfulness to God. Can people live faithfully for God in such times? The story of Ruth suggests they can.

❯ Read Ruth 4

The background to verses 3-4 is found in **Leviticus 25 v 25-28**. If poverty forced someone to sell their land, then a relative had the right to redeem that land in the future. It meant land remained in the family long-term. The guardian-redeemer was the relative who would act on behalf of the family in this way.

2. What would be the effects of this law?

Verses 4-6: The kinsman welcomes the opportunity to acquire more land for his family from a relative with no heirs. But then Boaz reveals that the kinsman must also marry Ruth to produce an heir for Elimelek, so the property can remain in Elimelek's family long-term. This means the kinsman is not buying land for himself, but redeeming land for his relatives. The kinsman therefore declines to do either, leaving the way free for Boaz to be the guardian-redeemer.

3. What is the prayer of the elders in verses 11-12?

4. According to verses 18-22, how is the prayer of the elders answered?

5. According to **Matthew 1 v 1-17** (see especially verse 5), how is the prayer of the elders answered?

6. The events of the book of Ruth happen "in the days when the judges ruled" (1 v 1). What were those days like? **See Judges 21 v 25.**

The days of the judges were a time of national unfaithfulness. Yet, in Bethlehem, the picture is very different.

7. Look back over the story of Ruth. Recall the ways in which we have seen God's people being faithful to God.

⤷ apply

8. How does the story of Ruth address the question of how we can be faithful in faithless times?

9. How does the end of the story of Ruth give hope for people living in faithless times?

⊡ getting personal

Think about situations in which you may find it particularly hard to remain faithful to God. Imagine yourself in those situations. Think about God's faithfulness to you. Think about His promises to you.

10. The women praise God because He "has not left you without a guardian-redeemer". The law of redemption, which is so beautifully illustrated in the story of Ruth, was a picture of Jesus our Redeemer. Complete the table.

Boaz the guardian-redeemer	Jesus our guardian-redeemer
Boaz publicly fulfilled all the legal requirements of redemption.	Romans 3 v 25-26 Galatians 3 v 13-14
For Boaz, being the guardian-redeemer involved personal cost.	1 Peter 1 v 18-19
For Boaz, redemption led to marriage.	Ephesians 5 v 25-27
Boaz provided an inheritance for Elimelek's family.	Hebrews 9 v 15

11. Think of Naomi at the beginning of the story. What did she think about her suffering? What purpose could she see in it?

12. Think of Naomi at the end of the story. What do you imagine she now thinks about her suffering? What purpose might she see in it?

→ apply

13. Think of times when God has used your suffering for a purpose. How can you encourage yourself to believe in God's goodness and purposes when you are going through difficult times?

↑ pray

1. Use your answers to Q10 to give thanks to God for Jesus our Redeemer.

2. Pray for those working or living in situations where it is especially hard to remain faithful to God.

3. Pray that those you know who are suffering might trust God even when they cannot see His purpose in their suffering.

Poverty and plenty

Ruth

LEADER'S GUIDE

Leader's Guide

INTRODUCTION

Leading a Bible study can be a bit like herding cats—everyone has a different idea of what the passage could be about, and a different line of enquiry that they want to pursue. But a good group leader is more than someone who just referees this kind of discussion. You will want to:

- correctly understand and handle the Bible passage. But also…

- encourage and train the people in your group to do this for themselves. Don't fall into the trap of spoon-feeding people by simply passing on the information in the Leader's Guide. Then…

- make sure that no Bible study is finished without everyone knowing how the passage is relevant for them. What changes do you all need to make in the light of the things you have been learning? And finally…

- encourage the group to turn all that has been learned and discussed into prayer.

Your Bible-study group is unique, and you are likely to know better than anyone the capabilities, backgrounds and circumstances of the people you are leading. That's why we've designed these guides with a number of optional features. If they're a quiet bunch, you might want to spend longer on talkabout. If your time is limited, you can choose to skip explore more, or get people to look at these questions at home. Can't get enough of Bible study? Well, some studies have optional extra homework projects. As leader, you can adapt and select the material to the needs of your particular group.

So what's in the Leader's Guide? The main thing that this Leader's Guide will help you to do is to understand the major teaching points in the passage you are studying, and how to apply them. As well as guidance on the questions, the Leader's Guide for each session contains the following important sections:

THE BIG IDEA

One key sentence will give you the main point of the session. This is what you should be aiming to have fixed in people's minds as they leave the Bible study. And it's the point you need to head back towards when the discussion goes off at a tangent.

SUMMARY

An overview of the passage, including plenty of useful historical background information.

OPTIONAL EXTRA

Usually this is an introductory activity that ties in with the main theme of the Bible study, and is designed to "break the ice" at the beginning of a session. Or it may be a "homework project" that people can tackle during the week.

So let's take a look at the various different features of a Good Book Guide:

⊕ talkabout

Each session kicks off with a discussion question, based on the group's opinions or experiences. It's designed to get people talking and thinking in a general way about the main subject of the Bible study.

⊕ investigate

The first thing you and your group need to know is what the Bible passage is about, which is the purpose of these questions. But watch out—people may come up with answers based on their experiences or teaching they have heard in the past, without referring to the passage at all. It's amazing how often we can get through a Bible study without actually looking at the Bible! If you're stuck for an answer, the Leader's Guide contains guidance on questions. These are the answers to direct your group to. This information isn't meant to be read out to people—ideally, you want them to discover these answers from the Bible for themselves. Sometimes there are optional follow-up questions (see ☑ in guidance on questions) to help you help your group get to the answer.

⊡ explore more

These questions generally point people to other relevant parts of the Bible. They are useful for helping your group to see how the passage fits into the "big picture" of the whole Bible. These sections are OPTIONAL—only use them if you have time. Remember that it's better to finish in good time having really grasped one big thing from the passage, than to try and cram everything in.

⊖ apply

We want to encourage you to spend more time working at application—too often, it is simply tacked on at the end. In the Good Book Guides, apply sections are mixed in with the investigate sections of the study. We hope that people will realise that application is not just an optional extra, but rather, the whole purpose of studying the

Bible. We do Bible study so that our lives can be changed by what we hear from God's word. If you skip the application, the Bible study hasn't achieved its purpose.

These questions draw out practical lessons that we can all learn from the Bible passage. You can review what has been learned so far, and think about practical differences that this should make in our churches and our lives. The group gets the opportunity to talk about what they personally have learned.

⊡ getting personal

These can be done at home, but it is well worth allowing a few moments of quiet reflection during the study for each person to think and pray about specific changes they need to make in their own lives. Why not have a time for reporting back at the beginning of the following session, so that everyone can be encouraged and challenged by one another to make application a priority?

⊕ pray

In Acts 4 v 25-30 the first Christians quoted Psalm 2 as they prayed in response to the persecution of the apostles by the Jewish religious leaders. Today however, it's not as common for Christians to base prayers on the truths of God's word as it once was. As a result, our prayers tend to be weak, superficial and self-centred rather than bold, visionary and God-centred.

The prayer section is based on what has been learned from the Bible passage. How different our prayer times would be if we were genuinely responding to what God has said to us through His word.

1 Ruth 1 – 2
A HIDDEN HAND

THE BIG IDEA
God rules over His people even if His actions are often hidden from us.

SUMMARY
• **Chapter 1:** In the book of Ruth an Israelite couple, Elimelek and Naomi, escape famine by emigrating to Moab with their two sons, even though the Israelites had been warned not to associate with the Moabites. In Moab the sons marry Moabite women, Orpah and Ruth. But Elimelek and his sons die, leaving Naomi, Orpah and Ruth as widows. Hearing that the famine is over in Israel, Naomi decides to return home and Ruth insists on returning with her.

• **Chapter 2:** To care for her mother-in-law, Ruth goes out gleaning (collecting any harvest left by the harvesters). She gleans in the fields of Boaz, who is kind and protective towards her.

• **Chapter 3:** Naomi knows that Boaz is a relative who could be entitled to marry Ruth and redeem the family's land. She tells Ruth to go to Boaz at night and invite him to marry her as her guardian-redeemer.

• **Chapter 4:** Boaz marries her after first dealing with the claims of a nearer relative, and together they give birth to a son.

• **This session:** Naomi recognises God's hand in her afflictions (1 v 13, 20). She has returned from Moab empty. Naomi means "pleasant", but now she wants to be known as Mara or "bitter". In chapter 2 the fortunes of Naomi and Ruth begin to change. At first the writer does not explicitly tell us that God is at work. But he recounts a series of "coincidences". We are invited to detect the hidden hand of God in

what unfolds. In 2 v 20 Naomi realises that God is at work. God rules over His people even if His actions are often hidden from us. The theological term for this is God's "providence".

OPTIONAL EXTRA
Read the whole of the book of Ruth aloud together in one sitting. You could ask four people to each read a chapter, but do not break it up so much that you lose a sense of the whole. Alternatively, you could show the animation of Ruth in the series *Testament: The Bible in Animation* (1996, S4C). At the end ask people the following questions:
• **What struck you about the story?**
• **What impression did the story make on you?**
• **What resonance does the story have with your life?**
• **What does the story show us about God?**

GUIDANCE ON QUESTIONS
1. At what times in your life have you found it hard to trust God? You might like to be ready with your own experience to share, to get discussion started. It's worth returning to this theme after Q12, and asking the group how what they've seen in Ruth 1 – 2 will help them next time they're finding it hard to trust God.

2. How did Elimelek respond to famine? See verse 1. Elimelek responded by emigrating to Moab.

3. How should the people of Israel have understood their famine? How should they have responded? Moses says in Deuteronomy 32 that God will send famine (v 23-24) when the people reject Him (v 15-18). But Moses also promises that God will have compassion on His people. Elimelek and the rest of the people should have responded to famine with repentance. Elimelek means "God is King". But Elimelek did not act as if God is King. Instead he turned from God to seek material blessing away from God's place of blessing. Bethlehem means "house of bread". The irony is that Elimelek left the "house of bread" to find bread.

4. What was the problem with going to Moab and marrying Moabite women? During the time of Judges, when the story of Ruth takes place (1 v 1), the Moabites oppressed Israel for 18 years (Judges 3 v 12-14). God had forbidden contact with the Moabites and intermarriage with the worshippers of other gods. The Moabites, the descendants of Lot (Deuteronomy 2 v 9), worshipped the god Chemosh, to whom human sacrifices were made. "Mahlon" and "Kilion" are Canaanite names.

5. Imagine what going back with Naomi meant for Ruth. Ruth faced continuing bereavement and widowhood, prejudice against immigrants, vulnerability to violence, dependence on charity and the responsibility of caring for her embittered mother-in-law.

6. How does Ruth show the covenant love of the Lord in her attitude to Naomi? Ruth shows love and loyalty to Naomi at great cost to herself, just as God shows love and loyalty to us at the cost of His own Son. (Orpah in contrast means "back of the neck" = "one who turns".)

7. How did Naomi describe what has happened to her in v 20-21? Naomi says

her life has become bitter. She uses names to describe her experience in Moab. Mahlon and Kilion mean "sickly" and "failing" (1 v 2). Naomi means pleasant, but Naomi's new chosen name, Mara, means "bitter".

8. Who does Naomi blame her misfortune on? Was she right to do this? Naomi says her misfortune comes from the LORD. It is not clear whether Naomi regards her misfortune as God's just judgment or unjust affliction. Calling herself Mara or "bitter" might suggest she resents God's action, but it might describe her circumstances rather than her attitude. "The LORD has afflicted me" in verse 21 means "The LORD has testified against me", which suggests she recognises the justice of God's judgment. By attributing her misfortune to God's hand, she is not denying her own responsibility. What is clear is that she sees her circumstances as God's work (v 13).

9. APPLY: What should hardship produce in our lives? Hardship should produce perseverance, character and hope in those who stand in grace.

How can we ensure that hardship produces perseverance, character and hope in our lives and not bitterness? Look at Romans 5 v 1-5 for your answers.

10. How do we see God's hand changing the circumstances of Naomi and Ruth? This is an opportunity for people to retell the story in their own words and to begin to pick out the signs of God at work.

11. Look at verses 12 and 20. What is said about the LORD in chapter 2? God is the one who gives refuge, just like a mother bird covering her chicks with her wing. "Kindness" in verse 20 is the word for 'covenant love' again. The LORD is the one who provides for His people in faithfulness to His covenant promises.

12. APPLY: What encouragement does this story give you for your circumstances? Ruth, Naomi and Boaz do not know the outcome of the events in which they are involved. And that is our normal experience. But in the book of Ruth we are allowed to view the story from God's perspective, with the outcome certain. We will gasp and sigh at the ups and downs of the story, but we know where it is going and we know who is in control. We cannot often view our lives from the perspective of God's sovereignty, but we can transfer the experience of reading Ruth to our lives. We will gasp and sigh at the ups and downs of our story, but we know where it is going and we know who is in control.

2 Ruth 2
A LIBERATING WORD

THE BIG IDEA
God's word creates an attractive community of kindness.

SUMMARY
The old covenant law given through Moses made provision for widows and refugees. The story of Ruth is a case study for these laws. It shows what happens when God's people obey the letter of the law in the spirit of the law. The result is protection and provision for a widowed refugee. In contrast to the enslaving rule of Pharaoh in Egypt, the law of God is liberating.

A key theme of the book of Ruth is loving-kindness, covenant love or loyalty (the Hebrew word is *hesed*). It describes the loyalty to the obligations of a covenant or agreement, and the generous spirit that is willing to go beyond those obligations. It is, for example, the love that wants to make both the legal commitment of marriage, and to make commitments in that relationship beyond any legal requirements.

In 2 v 20 Naomi blesses God for His "kindness". The refrain of Psalm 136 is "his love endures for ever" (= His covenant love or loyalty). God's people are to show the same kindness towards other people, especially the vulnerable. When they do, the community of God's people is an attractive community that commends God and His rule to the nations. Ruth is an example of this. She is a Moabite who finds refuge under God's wings (2 v 12).

GUIDANCE ON QUESTIONS
1. Recall an act of kindness that someone has done for you recently. Allow people to tell their stories. Then ask the group how these acts of kindness made them feel about God. Did they thank God for His kindness through other people? It might be appropriate to give thanks in prayer at this point.

2. What threats did Ruth face as a widow and refugee in a strange country? See verses 9, 15 and 22. Ruth was vulnerable to sexual harassment, verbal abuse, violence and exploitation.

3. Summarise what is commanded. How is this law fulfilled in the story of Ruth? God's people are to treat the vulnerable without partiality and care for them. Ruth is a widow and a refugee. But she is protected and provided for without prejudice. (See also Exodus 22 v 22-24; Leviticus 19 v 32-33; Numbers 15 v 15-16; Deuteronomy 14 v 28-29; 24 v 17; 26 v 12.)

4. Summarise what is commanded. How is this law fulfilled in the story of Ruth? See also Leviticus 19 v 9-10. Landowners were not to go over the harvest to gather what had been missed first time round, so that the poor could provide for themselves without recourse to undignified and dependence-generating charity.

5. What do we learn about the character of Ruth from these verses? Ruth takes the initiative to care for Naomi (v 2, 11) and works hard doing so (v 7). She is also humble (v 10, 13).

6. What do we learn about the character of Boaz from these verses? Boaz acknowledges the Lᴏʀᴅ and naturally turns to God in prayer (v 4, 12). He cares for the vulnerable (v 8-9) and anticipates their needs (v 14-16).

7. How do we see people expressing loving-kindness that goes beyond the letter of the law in Ruth 2? Ruth gleans to provide for her mother-in-law, but Boaz's foreman comments on her hard work (v 7, 11). Ruth has already remained loyal to Naomi despite Naomi's protestations (1 v 15-18). Boaz not only allows Ruth to glean in his fields, but invites her to continue doing so (v 8). Boaz provides water and food for Ruth (v 9, 14). Boaz instructs his men deliberately to leave barley unharvested for Ruth to collect (v 16).

EXPLORE MORE
The Israelites are to love aliens or refugees because they were once themselves aliens in Egypt. The rule of Egypt was harsh and oppressive, making them slaves. The law of God, by contrast, ensures that Ruth finds refuge and protection. It reveals a God who liberates and protects.

8. What kind of community does obedience to God create? Obedience to God's law creates an attractive community of kindness. See 1 Peter 2 v 9-12.

9. How does this fulfil God's promise to bless the nations through His people? God promised to Abraham that He would bless all nations through Abraham's family (Genesis 12 v 3). He said that, when the nation of Israel obeyed His law, the nations would see what a good God He was (Deuteronomy 4 v 5-8). The story of Ruth is a lovely picture of this in action. As God's people live under His rule in obedience to His law, a foreign widow finds provision and refuge.

3 Ruth 2 – 3
A WELCOMING COMMUNITY

THE BIG IDEA
God and His people provide a welcome for outsiders.

SUMMARY
If an Israelite man died without producing an heir, a relative was to marry his widow so that their first son could bear the name of the deceased man (Deuteronomy 25 v 5-10). (The technical term for this is "levirate marriage".) The nearest relative could refuse, but this was considered shameful. Naomi realises that under this law Boaz could marry Ruth, providing for her daughter-in-law and continuing Elimelek's family name. So in 3 v 1 she decides to build on Boaz's kindness so far.

Boaz may have been sleeping with the grain to prevent robbery before the harvest could be brought closer to home. Boaz did not recognise Ruth at first, perhaps because it was dark. We are not sure of the significance of raising the corner of Boaz's garment, but it seems to symbolise coming under his protection as her guardian-redeemer. There is nothing to suggest any sexual connotations or impropriety.

Boaz calls Ruth "daughter", which suggests there was a significant age gap between them (2 v 8; 3 v 10-11). Ruth could have married a younger man (3 v 10), but she offered herself to Boaz out of covenant faithfulness to Naomi and her family.

Boaz responds with the same covenant faithfulness. He knows a closer kinsman with a greater claim, but promises either to marry Ruth or act on her behalf. He also sends her on her way with a large quantity of barley as a sign of his willingness to act.

As a Moabite, Ruth is an outsider. But she is welcomed into God's community. God's wings of refuge are found through inclusion in the covenant community, as they are faithful to their covenant obligations in the spirit of covenant love. The word "home" in 3 v 1 is literally "rest". It is an image of salvation (Matthew 11 v 28-30; Hebrews 4 v 1-11).

OPTIONAL EXTRA
1. The Refugee Council (www. refugeecouncil.org.uk) has information refuting common myths about refugees and asylum seekers. Use this information to create a "true or false" quiz. It also has refugee stories. Read one or two stories and ask people to imagine how it must feel to be a refugee. Use with questions 1 or 7.

2. Ask different groups to complete a "CV" or "profile" for the following groups, using the headings of age, employment, likes, dislikes, status, main activities and friends.
• a typical church-goer
• Jesus
• your average "man in the street"
• Ruth
Compare the results. Around whom are the culture and practices of your church built? Ask how your culture and practices might need to adapt to include and welcome people who are "different"?

GUIDANCE ON QUESTIONS
1. Describe a situation in which you felt like an outsider. How did it feel? Again, it is worth having your own story ready to

recount, to give others time to call theirs to mind. Introduce the reading of Ruth 2 – 3 by encouraging your group to remember the feeling of being an "outsider" as they hear what happens to Ruth (this leads into Q2).

2. Imagine how Ruth and Boaz felt at each stage of the story. This is an opportunity both to retell the story and to allow people to grasp the dramatic force of what happens. Boaz may have been sleeping with the grain to prevent robbery before it could be brought closer to home. Boaz did not recognise Ruth at first, perhaps because it was dark. There is nothing to suggest any sexual impropriety in what happens. Indeed Boaz is keen to avoid any such suggestion (3 v 14). Boaz knows a closer kinsman with a greater claim, but promises either to marry Ruth or act on her behalf. He sends her on her way with a large quantity of corn as a sign of his willingness to act.

3. What is the significance of how Ruth is described? The writer emphasises, through the frequent references to Ruth being from Moab, that she is a Gentile foreigner.

4. How were Moabites viewed in Israel? Moabites were not to be included among God's people because of their idolatry and human sacrifice. They were also oppressing God's people or had done so recently (Judges 3 v 12-14).

5. How does Ruth view God's people? Ruth embraces the Israelites as her own people and embraces God as her God.

6. How do we see Ruth being included among God's people? As we saw in the last session, Ruth is protected and provided for as God's people live in obedience to

God's law. In chapter 3 we begin to see how Ruth will find a home among God's people. The "wings of refuge" is a lovely statement of inclusion (2 v 12).

7. APPLY: What different attitudes do people have to refugees and immigrants? The town where you live, and the political/cultural climate you are in, will shape people's responses to this question. It may be that you need to use this question to challenge your group's assumptions and opinions about immigrants, based on your study of Ruth so far.

8. APPLY: What could you or your church do to provide a welcome for immigrants or other marginalised groups? Encourage people to answer this both as individuals and as a community.

9. What is the significance of the parallels between these two verses? Ruth comes under God's wings or garment of refuge as she comes under Boaz's wings or garment. Boaz discovers that he is the answer to his prayer of 2 v 12.

EXPLORE MORE
The inclusion and protection of Ruth by Boaz is a picture of God's relationship with His people. God graciously welcomes His people, with all our sin and shame, into a covenant relationship of love. We are to reflect God's gracious welcome to us in our attitude to outsiders (compare, for example, Luke 14 v 13 and 21).

10. APPLY: Can you think of times when you have discovered that you are God's answer to your prayer for someone? Depending on your group, the answer to this question may be "no", which is fine! If you know of someone in your group who has a really encouraging story to share in answer to this question, it might be worth asking them beforehand about it, so that they're prepared.

11. What do these verses tell us about the place of women in that culture?
Naomi says she has returned empty, though in fact she has returned with Ruth (1 v 21). But to Naomi, who has lost her husbands and sons, Ruth does not seem to count because she is only a woman. Women were regarded as someone's possession (2 v 5). They were vulnerable to harassment from men (2 v 9).

12. Look ahead to 4 v 15. What attitude about the value of women, counter cultural back then, is shown here?
Women should not be belittled or under-valued—their contribution can be greater than that of seven men. While Boaz and the men at the gate speak of one who will continue the name of Elimelek and Mahlon, the book climaxes with the women of the town speaking of one who will provide for Naomi.

EXPLORE MORE
Jesus reveals the radical grace of God in His willingness to socialise with sinners. Tax collectors were regarded as enemies of the nation and enemies of God because they collaborated with the Roman occupiers. But God eats with His enemies! Jesus has come for the lost. The Pharisees are scandalised because this undermines their status, respectability and self-righteousness.

13. APPLY: Who are the outsiders in your area? What does your church do to ensure they feel welcome? You may want to discuss the fact that sometimes we can say people are welcome, but make it hard for them to fit in. Does this have any implications for your group?

---

4 Ruth 4
A FAITHFUL REDEEMER

THE BIG IDEA
We can be faithful in faithless times because we have a faithful Redeemer.

SUMMARY
The background to verses 3-4 is found in Leviticus 25 v 25-28. If poverty forced someone to sell their land, then a relative had the right and responsibility to redeem that land in the future. It meant land remained in the family long-term. The "guardian-redeemer" was the relative who would act on behalf of the family in this way. The town gate was the place where business and legal matters were dealt with.

Why did Ruth go gleaning when Naomi owned property? It may have been a small, unviable piece of land. But also Naomi and Ruth returned when the harvest was beginning (1 v 22) so they had not been able to sow the land.

The nature of the proposed transaction in verses 3-4 is not entirely clear. Naomi could be selling her land and giving first option to her nearest guardian-redeemer, or she could be looking for the guardian-redeemer to sort out the outstanding issues of inheritance created by having no male heir.

The unnamed kinsman welcomes the opportunity to acquire more land for his family from a relative with no heirs. But then Boaz reveals that the kinsman must also marry Ruth to produce an heir for Elimelek so the property can remain in Elimelek's family long-term. This means the kinsman is not buying land for himself, but redeeming land for his relatives.

Boaz links the redemption of property with the duty of marriage to ensure the kinsman does not choose to marry Ruth. If the kinsman marries Ruth, he thereby acknowledges his responsibility to buy land that will not be his long-term. If he buys the land, he must pass it on to Elimelek's heir. So he declines to do either, leaving the way free for Boaz to act as guardian-redeemer. A sandal was used to ratify the transactions (v 7-8). It may have symbolised the right to walk the land as your own.

The law of redemption, which is so beautifully illustrated in the story of Ruth, is a picture of Jesus our Redeemer. Jesus redeems us from sin and provides us with an eternal inheritance because of His covenant love, fulfilling all the legal requirements and at the cost of His own life.

The story of Ruth takes place in the time of the judges (1 v 1). This was a time of widespread unfaithfulness to God. But Ruth and Boaz are faithful to God because God is faithful to His covenant. God is graciously using Ruth and Boaz to continue His plan of salvation through Jesus. The problem in the time of the judges was that "in those days Israel had no king; everyone did as he saw fit" (Judges 21 v 25). But the book of Ruth ends by showing that from Boaz and Ruth will come David—Israel's greatest king. Ruth is also mentioned in Matthew 1 v 5. Ultimately, from Ruth and Boaz comes

David's greater son, Jesus. Jesus is God's promised Saviour-King. We can live faithfully in a godless society, in times of moral chaos and confusion, because God still reigns, Christ is the King and God's saving purposes continue.

GUIDANCE ON QUESTIONS

1. How much easier or harder is it for young Christians to live faithfully for Christ than it was for previous generations? There are no "right answers" here! In many ways it seems to be harder to live as a Christian in the west: aggressive atheism; faith being seen as irrelevant; the way Christian morality is disappearing from policy and culture; some churches turning their backs on Scriptural teaching.
Your group may well find it easier to think of these than how it's easier to live as a Christian today, but here are a few suggestions: the internet means we have more access to good teaching, and are more easily able to keep in touch with Christians around the world; there is a clearer dividing line between Christians and non-Christians, and so less of a danger of nominal Christianity; our culture is becoming more like the world of the New Testament (non-Christian state, multicultural society, misunderstanding and persecution of Christians), so that the Bible speaks very clearly to our situation.

2. What would be the effects of this law? The law ensured that long-term a family always had land and, in a farming economy, that meant they always had a livelihood. If a guardian-redeemer could not redeem the land, then at the Year of Jubilee it would revert to the family in any case. In a sense, the buyer was purchasing a number of harvests on leasehold rather than buying the land itself. Behind this was a theological idea: the land belonged to God and He gave it as an inheritance to everyone in Israel. Redeeming your land meant regaining your inheritance from God and your place in the covenant community.

3. What is the prayer of the elders in verses 11-12? Rachel and Leah were the wives of Jacob and their sons were the patriarchs, who formed the twelve tribes of Israel. The elders therefore pray that Boaz and Ruth will produce many descendants, who will build up God's people.

Under the law concerning the marriage of widows, the first son carried the name of the deceased man. In marrying Ruth, Boaz was potentially giving up the future of his name for the sake of his deceased relative. So the elders pray that Boaz will be famous in his own right.

Note on Perez: In Genesis 38, Er, the first son of Judah (one of the twelve patriarchs), marries a woman called Tamar. Er, however, dies so Judah tells his second son, Onan, to fulfil his obligation to provide an heir for his brother by taking Tamar as his wife. But Onan does not have full intercourse with Tamar, to avoid producing an heir for his brother. As a result, the LORD kills him. Judah puts off taking any further action, fearing another son might die. So Tamar disguises herself as a prostitute and tricks Judah himself into sleeping with her. Judah is angry when he learns Tamar is pregnant, but then she dramatically reveals him to be the father. Judah declares her to be "more righteous than I" because she has taken seriously the obligation to provide an heir for Er. She gives birth to twins, one of whom is named Perez. Perez was therefore the result of the same kind of marital obligation that had brought Boaz and Ruth together. Perez had gone on to produce a notable line of descendants,

including most of those sitting at the town gate of Bethlehem.

4. According to verses 18-22, how is the prayer of the elders answered? The final word of the book of Ruth is "David". This is its climax. Readers in later generations would know how significant this was. David was Israel's greatest king and God promised David that one of his descendants would always reign over God's people (2 Samuel 7 v 12-13). Boaz, who gave up his name, goes down in history as the great-grandfather of King David, and Ruth, the refugee widow, goes down in history as the great-grandmother of King David.

5. According to the NT, how is the prayer of the elders answered? From the descendants of Boaz and Ruth comes God's promised Saviour-King. Christ builds up the house of Israel. In other words, He saves God's people and makes them a kingdom that includes people from all nations.

6. What were the days of the judges like? There was a cycle of sin, judgment, sorrow and restoration (see Judges 2). But at the end we are left with moral chaos and violence at every level: family, tribe and nation (Judges 17 – 21). People are making up their own religion and ethics (Judges 17 v 1-6). It is a society that has forgotten God's word (Judges 2 v 10).

7. How have we seen God's people being faithful? This book is a case study in OT law and the spirit of that law. A Moabite widow finds shelter among God's people as they live in accordance with His law.

8. APPLY: How does the story of Ruth address the question of how we can be faithful in faithless times? God's people can be faithful because God is faithful to His covenant promises. We have seen that God's people are to reflect God's covenant love or loving-kindness.

9. APPLY: How does the end of the story of Ruth give hope for people living in faithless times?

⌄

Compare the last verse of the book of the Judges with the last verse of the book of Ruth. The problem in Judges is that Israel had no king (Judges 21 v 25). But by the end of the book of Ruth, we discover that God's King is coming.

The answer to Judges 21 v 25 is God's rule and God's king. Ultimately, through the offspring of Ruth comes Jesus, David's greater son, the King of Israel and the King of the world. Through His rule He perfectly upholds and establishes God's rule of blessing, life, justice and peace. Just as Ruth the Moabitess becomes part of the covenant community, so today the gospel goes to all nations. God continues to bring men and women into His kingdom. Christ the King rules over all things, even over a godless society that refuses to acknowledge Him, and He orders all things for the good of His people. So we can live in a godless society, in times of moral chaos and confusion, because God still reigns, Christ is the King and God's saving purposes continue.

10. The law of redemption, which is so beautifully illustrated in the story of Ruth, was a picture of Jesus our Redeemer. Complete the table.
Boaz was willing to redeem because of his loving-kindness or covenant love. Jesus willingly lays down His life to redeem us

(John 10 v 11-13).
- **Legal requirements:** On the cross Jesus publicly pays the price of redemption.
- **Personal cost:** Jesus pays for our redemption with His own blood.
- **Marriage:** Jesus redeems His people to make them His bride.
- **Inheritance:** Jesus provides us with an eternal inheritance (see Hebrews 9 v 15).

11. What did Naomi think about her suffering? What purpose could she see in it? Naomi's sufferings leave her bitter and empty (1 v 20-21). She can see them as God's judgment (1 v 13, 21), but she cannot see any redemptive purpose in them.

12. What do you imagine she now thinks about her suffering? What purpose might she see in it? Look at 4 v 14-17. Naomi discovers through her suffering that she has a daughter-in-law "who is better to you than seven sons" (4 v 15). "Renew your life" in 4 v 15 is literally "return your soul": back in the covenant community Naomi is "full" again. She gains a purpose for her life (4 v 16) and an heir for her family (4 v 17). Yet, even with this, Naomi does not see the full purpose behind her suffering, for she does not know that God's King will come from her descendants.

OPTIONAL EXTRA
Try to summarise the Big Ideas (look back over the headings in the Leader's Guide) from Ruth and apply them specifically to both individuals and the life of your Christian community.
Ask group members to highlight one thing that they will, with God's help, seek to change as a result of reading this book.

Good Book Guides
The full range

Galatians: 7 Studies
Timothy Keller
ISBN: 9781908762559

Ephesians: 10 Studies
Thabiti Anyabwile
ISBN: 9781907377099

Ephesians: 8 Studies
Richard Coekin
ISBN: 9781910307694

Philippians: 7 Studies
Steven J. Lawson
ISBN: 9781784981181

Colossians: 6 Studies
Mark Meynell
ISBN: 9781906334246

1 Thessalonians:
7 Studies
Mark Wallace
ISBN: 9781904889533

2 Timothy: 7 Studies
Mark Mulryne
ISBN: 9781905564569

Titus: 5 Studies
Tim Chester
ISBN: 9781909919631

Hebrews: 8 Studies
Justin Buzzard
ISBN: 9781906334420

James: 6 Studies
Sam Allberry
ISBN: 9781910307816

1 Peter: 5 Studies
Tim Chester
ISBN: 9781907377853

1 Peter: 6 Studies
Juan R. Sanchez
ISBN: 9781784980177

1 John: 7 Studies
Nathan Buttery
ISBN: 9781904889953

Revelation 2–3: 7 Studies
Jonathan Lamb
ISBN: 9781905564682

TOPICAL

Man of God: 10 Studies
Anthony Bewes & Sam
Allberry
ISBN: 9781904889977

Biblical Womanhood:
10 Studies
Sarah Collins
ISBN: 9781907377532

The Apostles' Creed:
10 Studies
Tim Chester
ISBN: 9781905564415

**Promises Kept Bible
Overview:** 9 Studies
Carl Laferton
ISBN: 9781908317933

Contentment: 6 Studies
Anne Woodcock
ISBN: 9781905564668

**These truths alone: the
Reformation Solas**
6 Studies
Jason Helopoulos
ISBN: 9781784981501

Women of Faith:
8 Studies
Mary Davis
ISBN: 9781904889526

Meeting Jesus: 8 Studies
Jenna Kavonic
ISBN: 9781905564460

Heaven: 6 Studies
Andy Telfer
ISBN: 9781909919457

Making Work Work:
8 Studies
Marcus Nodder
ISBN: 9781908762894

The Holy Spirit: 8 Studies
Pete & Anne Woodcock
ISBN: 9781905564217

Experiencing God:
6 Studies
Tim Chester
ISBN: 9781906334437

Real Prayer: 7 Studies
Anne Woodcock
ISBN: 9781910307595

thegoodbook
COMPANY

BIBLICAL | RELEVANT | ACCESSIBLE

At The Good Book Company, we are dedicated to helping Christians and local churches grow. We believe that God's growth process always starts with hearing clearly what he has said to us through his timeless word—the Bible.

Ever since we opened our doors in 1991, we have been striving to produce resources that honor God in the way the Bible is used. We have grown to become an international provider of user-friendly resources to the Christian community, with believers of all backgrounds and denominations using our Bible studies, books, evangelistic resources, DVD-based courses, and training events.

We want to equip ordinary Christians to live for Christ day by day, and churches to grow in their knowledge of God, their love for one another, and the effectiveness of their outreach.

Call us for a discussion of your needs or visit one of our local websites for more information on the resources and services we provide.

Your friends at The Good Book Company

NORTH AMERICA
UK & EUROPE
AUSTRALIA
NEW ZEALAND

thegoodbook.com
thegoodbook.co.uk
thegoodbook.com.au
thegoodbook.co.nz

866 244 2165
0333 123 0880
(02) 9564 3555
(+64) 3 343 2463

WWW.CHRISTIANITYEXPLORED.ORG
Our partner site is a great place for those exploring the Christian faith, with a clear explanation of the good news, powerful testimonies and answers to difficult questions.